SCIENCE Workbook

Level 5

MOONSTONE

Published in Moonstone
by Rupa Publications India Pvt. Ltd 2022
7/16, Ansari Road, Daryaganj
New Delhi 110002

Sales centres:
Allahabad Bengaluru Chennai
Hyderabad Jaipur Kathmandu
Kolkata Mumbai

ISBN: 978-93-5520-698-5

First impression 2022

10 9 8 7 6 5 4 3 2 1

Printed in India

Contents

Growing Plants 4

Animals and Their Features 7

Skeletal System 10

Nervous System 13

Food and Health 16

Safety and First-Aid 19

Rocks and Minerals 22

Light and Shadow 25

Force 28

Energy 31

Environmental Pollution 34

Natural Phenomena 37

The Earth, Sun and Moon 40

The Solar System 44

Answers 47

Growing Plants

1. Fill in the blanks with the correct option.

a. Most plants grow from ________________. (leaves/seeds)

b. Plants that are grown in large quantity during a particular season are called ________________. (crops/agriculture)

c. Terrace farming is done on ________________. (mountains/rivers)

d. The seed gets its food from the ________________. (bud/ cotyledons)

e. Birds and bees help in the ________________ of seeds. (agriculture/ dispersal)

2. Write T for true statements and F for the false ones.

a. Germination is important for growing a new plant. ☐

b. All the seeds are similar in shape and size. ☐

c. For a healthy plant, we should sow many seeds at the same place. ☐

d. Manure provides nutrients to soil to increase its fertility. ☐

e. Only food crops should be grown in large quantity. ☐

3. Number the sentences to show the stages of agriculture.

a. Irrigation of crops. ☐

b. Ploughing the soil. ☐

c. Adding fertilizers to the soil. ☐

d. Harvesting the crops. ☐

e. Sowing seeds in the field. ☐

4. Match the following.

Plant	Reproductive Part
a. Coconut	Eyes
b. Potato	Leaf
c. Rose	Roots
d. Carrot	Stem
e. Bryophyllum	Seed

5. Name two plants which disperse their seeds by:

a. Explosion ____________________, ____________________

b. Wind ____________________, ____________________

c. Animal Agents ____________________, ____________________

d. Water ____________________, ____________________

6. Answer the following questions.

a. What is germination?

____

____

b. What do you mean by the agents of dispersal?

____

____

c. Why do farmers use insecticides and pesticides?

____

____

d. Describe the structure of a seed.

e. What are the three main kinds of crops?

7. Think and write

Organic farming is a system which avoids the use of synthetic materials and promotes the use of only biological products for agriculture. Write a short note on the need of organic farming.

8. Activity time

You eat different kinds of fruits in different seasons. Instead of throwing away the seeds in the dustbin, sow them in your garden and grow your own plants. Remember, a plant takes many years to grow into a big tree.

Animals and Their Features

1. Fill in the blanks.

a. ________________ have sharp canines and strong jaws.

b. An alligator lives in a ________________.

c. Snakes have ________________ on their body.

d. ________________ habitat is a large water body with salty water.

e. Walrus is found in ________________ habitat.

2. Write T for true statements and F for false ones.

a. Snakes use their hind limbs to crawl. ☐

b. Camels store water in their hump. ☐

c. Penguins can swim, walk and fly easily. ☐

d. Birds have solid bones to help them fly. ☐

e. Chameleon can change its body colour to hide in its surroundings. ☐

3. Name two animals which have the following body part:

a. Shell ________________, ________________

b. Spine ________________, ________________

c. Fur ________________, ________________

d. Feathers ________________, ________________

e. Flippers ________________, ________________

4. Name two animals which belong to the following habitat:

a. Desert ____________, ____________

b. Ocean ____________, ____________

c. Forest ____________, ____________

d. Polar ____________, ____________

e. Mountain ____________, ____________

5. Short answer questions.

a. Define habitat.

____

b. Animals of which habitat have webbed feet?

____

c. Name the group of animals which can live both on land and in water.

____

d. Which organ is used by the snakes to move?

____

e. Name the different organs used by animals to breathe.

____

f. Name two animals which breathe through their skin.

____

6. Long answer questions.

a. What is adaptation?

____

____

b. What are the features of animals living in the polar region?

c. Why do some animals have sharp teeth?

d. What are the different food habits of animals?

7. Think and write

Animals have different organs for movement which help them move in different ways. Write how have they adapted to move differently?

8. Activity time

Some animals like lizards and frogs go into deep sleep for a long period of time. Collect more data about animal hibernation and make a project explaining the migration of any one animal.

Skeletal System

1. Choose the correct answer.

a. Which part of the bone protects the brain?

Vertebrae ☐ Skull ☐

b. The joint at the top of our neck.

Gliding ☐ Pivotal ☐

c. The place where blood cells are produced.

Bone marrow ☐ Cartilage ☐

d. The tissues which connect muscles to the bones.

Ligament ☐ Tendons ☐

e. The name of ring like bones.

Girdle ☐ Hinge ☐

2. Write T for true statements and F for false ones.

a. There are more than 206 bones in our body. ☐

b. The lower jaw bone is not fixed and hence can move. ☐

c. Most of the joints in our body are immovable. ☐

d. The soft bones in our body produce blood cells. ☐

3. Short answer questions.

a. Name the part of the skeletal system that protects our heart.

____

b. What is the other name of the backbone?

____

c. How many girdles are present in our body?

____

d. Where is the spinal cord located?

____

e. Which type of joint is present in our shoulder?

____

f. Which type of joint is present in our knees?

____

g. What is the function of the ligaments in the skeletal system?

____

4. Match the name of the joints to their feature.

Column A	Column B
a. Ball and socket joint	Back and forth movement
b. Hinge joint	Joints in our wrist
c. Pivot joint	Elbow joint
d. Gliding joint	Connects the head to the neck

5. Long answer questions.

a. What are the functions of the skeletal system?

____

____

b. What is sternum? Name the bones attached to it.

c. What are joints? Name the various types of joints present in our body.

d. What is the function of cartilage in our body?

6. Think and write

Our backbone is made up of 33 small bones. Imagine if this bone was made up of a long bone instead of small bones. Write the activities which you won't be able to perform in such a case.

7. Activity Time

Find out the different diseases related to bones which are common in your country. Try to find the causes and symptoms of these diseases.

Nervous System

1. Choose the correct answer.

a. The largest part of the human brain.

Cerebrum ☐ Medulla ☐

b. Which organ is not a part of the nervous system?

Spinal cord ☐ Hair ☐

c. The part of the nervous system that controls reflex actions.

Cerebellum ☐ Spinal cord ☐

d. The part of the brain that controls heartbeat.

Medulla ☐ Cerebrum ☐

e. These run throughout our body to form a network.

Spinal cord ☐ Nerves ☐

2. Write T for true statements and F for false ones.

a. The brain is the control centre of our body. ☐

b. The medulla controls our heartbeat and sneezing. ☐

c. Reflex actions are controlled by the organs. ☐

d. The sense organs are controlled by the spinal cord. ☐

3. Short answer questions.

a. Name the organs of the nervous system.

____

b. Name three parts of the brain.

____

c. What is the function of sensory nerves?

____

d. What is the function of motor nerves?

____

e. Name the five sense organs.

____

f. What is a reflex action?

____

g. What are ligaments?

____

4. Match the senses to the part of the sensory organ they relate to.

Column A	Column B
a. See	Eardrum
b. Feel	Taste buds
c. Hear	Skin
d. Smell	Pupil
e. Taste	Nostrils

5. Long answer questions.

a. What is the primary function of the nervous system?

____

____

b. What is the function of cerebrum?

c. What activities are controlled by the medulla?

d. Give an example of reflex action.

6. Think and write

Our backbone surrounds and protects the spinal cord. Why does the spinal cord need protection?

7. Activity Time

Our ears also contain small bones which help us to hear the sounds. Find out how these bones sense and translate audio signals.

Food and Health

1. Choose the correct answer.

a. It provides energy to the body.

Cereals ☐ Grapes ☐

b. The disease which can spread from an infected to a healthy person.

Measles ☐ Cancer ☐

c. The disease which is non-communicable.

Tuberculosis ☐ Goitre ☐

d. It is a good source of roughage.

Corns ☐ Milk ☐

e. A type of medicine taken to prevent specific diseases.

Antibiotic ☐ Vaccine ☐

2. Write T for true statements and F for false ones.

a. Water should be allowed to stagnate around the house. ☐

b. Common cold can be prevented by taking vaccine. ☐

c. Goitre is caused by the deficiency of iodine in our diet. ☐

d. Roughage is important to avoid dehydration. ☐

e. We should maintain hygiene to stay healthy. ☐

3. Write the antonyms of the words in brackets to complete the sentences.

a. ________________ posture is essential for staying healthy. (Incorrect)

b. We should eat ________________ and healthy food. (dirty)

c. Mosquitoes breed in ________________ water. (flowing)

d. We should stay away from an ________________ person. (healthy)

e. Food, kept ________________, should not be eaten. (covered)

4. Complete the table given below.

Deficiency disease	Cause of disease	Food to prevent deficiency
a. Scurvy		
b. Beriberi		
c. Night blindness		
d. Anaemia		
e. Goitre		

5. Short answer questions.

a. Define disease.

____

b. Name the important components of food.

____

c. Name two communicable diseases.

____

d. Name two non-communicable diseases.

____

e. Name two deficiency diseases.

____

f. Define hygiene.

____

6. Long answer questions.

a. What is the importance of a balanced diet?

____

____

b. What is the cause of deficiency disease? How can we avoid them?

____

____

c. How do communicable diseases spread?

____

____

d. Why should we get vaccinated?

____

____

7. Think and write

Mandy has caught measles and her younger brother uses the same blanket as she does. Think and write the consequences of doing this.

____

____

____

____

____

8. Activity time

List down the names of the food items you ate yesterday. Now write the names of the minerals and vitamin your body received. Categorise your meal as balanced or unbalanced on the basis of the data.

Safety and First-Aid

1. Fill in the blanks.

a. A ________________ occurs when a joint gets twisted and swells up.

b. Severe burns should only be treated by a ________________.

c. A ________________ bite can be poisonous.

d. Throwing ________________ on fire cuts off the air supply and puts it off.

e. We should open doors and windows in case of ________________.

2. Write T for true statements and F for the false ones.

a. A break or crack in muscle is called fracture. ☐

b. A bee sting can be cured at home. ☐

c. A blister must not be pricked. ☐

d. Switching on lights in case of gas leak can be dangerous. ☐

e. Electrical faults cannot cause fire. ☐

3. Answer the following in one word.

a. An instrument used to put out fire. ________________

b. An immediate help given to an injured person. ________________

c. A home remedy for wasp stings. ________________

d. A support to hold the fracture in place. ________________

e. It should be applied on a sprain. ________________

4. Short answer questions.

a. What do you mean by first-aid?

____

b. What is a fracture?

____

c. How can we avoid infections in case of cuts or scratches?

____

d. Name a disease caused by insect bites.

____

e. What is a blister?

____

f. How can small fires be put out?

____

5. Long answer questions.

a. What are the different causes of fire?

____

____

b. What first-aid should be given in case of a fractured limb?

____

____

c. What should you do in case of nose bleed?

____

____

d. What should be done in case of a gas leak?

____

____

6. Think and write

In public places such as shopping malls, banks and schools, various safety drills are organized time to time. Explain how a safety drill is helpful for us.

____

____

____

____

____

7. Activity time

Find out the phone numbers of local helpline services such as fire station, police station, ambulance service etc. Also find the emergency helpline number of your city and memorise it.

Rocks and Minerals

1. Choose the correct answer.

a. The innermost layer of Earth is

Core ☐ Crust ☐

b. A glassy igneous rock.

Pumice ☐ Obsidian ☐

c. A soft stone which is red in colour.

Sandstone ☐ Shale ☐

d. Marble is formed from this rock.

Limestone ☐ Shale ☐

e. This substance can be attracted by a magnet.

Sapphire ☐ Iron ☐

2. Write T for true statements and F for false ones.

a. Minerals are also used to make jewels and ornaments. ☐

b. Diamond is the softest mineral. ☐

c. Minerals are made up of rocks. ☐

d. Igneous rocks are the first rocks formed on the Earth. ☐

e. Coal is also called a fossil fuel. ☐

3. Give two examples for the following.

a. Igneous rocks ______________, ______________

b. Sedimentary rocks ____________, ____________

c. Metamorphic rocks ____________, ____________

d. Metallic minerals ____________, ____________

e. Non-metallic minerals ____________, ____________

4. Match the following.

Rock	**Property**
a. Shale	Rich in mineral quartz
b. Gneiss	Hard rock formed by lava
c. Quartzite	Thin layers of solidified clay
d. Granite	Porous rock
e. Pumice	Formed from granite

5. Short answer questions.

a. Name three types of rocks.

____

b. Name three layers of the Earth?

____

c. What are the uses of limestone?

____

d. Name some minerals which are a part of our diet.

____

e. Which minerals are called fossil fuels?

____

f. Name the igneous rock which has holes in it.

____

6. Long answer questions.

a. How are igneous rocks formed?

____

____

b. What are sedimentary rocks?

____

____

c. What are magnets? Mention their types with examples.

____

____

d. How are metamorphic rocks formed?

____

____

7. Think and write

Different types of rocks are used as building materials. Look around your house and school and write the names of the rocks used for construction.

____

____

____

____

____

8. Activity time

Use an atlas to find the places where different types of rocks and minerals are found in your country.

Light and Shadow

1. Fill in the blanks with the correct word.

a. Wood is an ________________ object. (translucent/opaque)

b. Transparent objects do not block ________________. (light/shadow)

c. A shadow is always ________________. (black/colourful)

d. ________________ is a natural luminous object. (Torch/Sun)

e. A shadow is ________________ early in the morning. (short/long)

2. Write the names of the given objects in the correct column.

Torch	Wooden chair	Plastic bottle	Lamp
Water	Mirror	Sun	Fire

Luminous objects	Non-luminous objects

3. Define the following terms.

a. Luminous ____

____

b. Non-luminous ____

____

c. Transparent ______________________________

____

d. Translucent ______________________________

____

e. Opaque ______________________________

____

4. Name two objects which are:

a. Luminous ______________, ______________

b. Non-luminous ______________, ______________

c. Transparent ______________, ______________

d. Translucent ______________, ______________

e. Opaque ______________, ______________

5. Answer the questions given below.

a. How are shadows formed?

____

____

b. What are the similarities between the shadow of a human and that of a tree?

____

____

c. Where does a shadow form and why?

____

d. What are the essential conditions for a shadow to form?

6. Think and write

Observe your shadow at different times in a day. Think and write why the length and position of the shadow changes throughout the day.

7. Activity time

Use a torch in a dark room to form shadows using your hands. Try to form shadows that look like animals and other objects.

Force

1. Fill in the blanks with the correct option.

a. Force can ______________ a stationary object. (move/stop)

b. Force can change the ______________ of an object. (name/shape)

c. ______________ is used to reduce friction. (Pebbles/Oil)

d. The ______________ force attracts objects towards the centre of the Earth. (magnetic/gravitational)

e. Friction acts in the ______________ direction to the direction of applied force. (opposite/same)

2. Write T for true statements and F for false ones.

a. Force can change the shape of an object. ☐

b. Electrostatic force is not useful at all. ☐

c. Gravity is the cause of magnetic force of attraction. ☐

d. The effect of forces on objects can be seen. ☐

e. Frictional force acts in the same direction as of applied force. ☐

3. Give an example of the following.

a. Gravitational force ______________________________

b. Frictional force ______________________________

c. Magnetic force ______________________________

d. Mechanical force ______________________________

e. Buoyant force ______________________________

4. Match the following.

Column A	Column B
a. Friction	Pulling force of Earth
b. Magnetism	Upward force
c. Gravity	Used to attract metals
d. Force	Slows down movement
e. Buoyant	Push or pull

5. Short answer questions.

a. What are the effects of force on a stationary object?

____

b. What are the effects of force on a moving object?

____

c. Why is gravitational force important for a planet?

____

d. What do you understand by magnetism?

____

e. Why do we need to oil machine parts?

____

6. Long answer questions.

a. List two advantages of frictional force.

____

____

b. List two disadvantages of frictional force.

c. What is buoyant force? Give an example.

d. What are the advantages of buoyant force?

7. Think and write

Observe the different forces in action while you play different games. Explain when and why you needed to exert more force during your game.

8. Activity time

Take a tub and fill it partially with water. Put an open piece of aluminium foil on water. Now take another piece of aluminium foil and fold its corners to make a boat and put it in water too. Now put one pebbles or coin on both the foils. Observe what happens and why.

Energy

1. Fill in the blanks.

a. We need ________________ energy to cook food.

b. The heat energy from the Earth is called ________________ energy.

c. A computer needs ________________ energy to work.

d. A scissor is an example of ________________ lever.

e. Lamps are used as the source of ________________ energy.

2. Write T for true statements and F for false ones.

a. A bottle-opener is an example of first-class lever. ☐

b. Energy can be changed from one form to another. ☐

c. Wheel and axle move together. ☐

d. Inclined planes are also a type of lever. ☐

e. Coal and petroleum are examples of fossil fuels. ☐

3. Give two examples of the following.

a. Renewable energy ________________, ________________

b. Non-renewable energy ________________, ________________

c. First-class lever ________________, ________________

d. Second-class lever ________________, ________________

e. Third-class lever ________________, ________________

f. Wedge ________________, ________________

g. Uses of screw ________________, ________________

h. Inclined plane ______________, ______________

4. Match the following.

Column A	Column B
a. Dams	Electrical energy
b. Windmills	Sound energy
c. Solar panels	Solar energy
d. Drums and trumpets	Hydro energy
e. Electrical appliances	Wind energy

5. Short answer questions.

a. Define energy.

____

b. What is renewable energy?

____

c. What is non-renewable energy?

____

d. Name six simple machines.

____

e. What are the three parts of a lever?

____

f. Write two examples where we use heat energy.

____

g. Write two activities in which we use sound energy.

____

6. Long answer questions.

a. Why do we need simple machines?

b. Explain the use of all the three parts of a lever?

c. Differentiate between a fixed and a movable pulley.

d. What is a wheel and axle? Give two examples.

7. Think and write

People around the world have reduced the use of non-renewable sources of energy to protect our environment. Solar energy, wind energy and geothermal energy are given preference. Think and write why.

8. Activity time

Identify complex machines which include simple machines in them. Draw or paste their pictures in your activity file and write their name.

Environmental Pollution

1. Fill in the blanks.

a. Vehicles and industries are a major cause of ________________ pollution.

b. Waste released into water bodies cause ________________ pollution.

c. Loud noises from loudspeakers can damage our ________________.

d. Soil erosion is caused by ________________.

e. We should reduce the use of ________________ fuels.

2. Write T for true statements and F for false ones.

a. We should use polythene bags to save our environment. ☐

b. We should plant more trees to reduce global warming. ☐

c. Ozone layer causes skin cancer. ☐

d. Soil erosion is caused by heavy rains. ☐

e. Volcanoes also cause air pollution when they erupt. ☐

4. Short answer questions.

a. Define environment.

____

b. What is the major cause of acid rain?

____

c. What is global warming?

____

d. What is deforestation?

____

e. Why is ozone layer important for us?

____

f. What is soil erosion?

____

4. Complete the table given below.

Air Pollution	
Causes	Effects
Water Pollution	
Causes	Effects
Land Pollution	
Causes	Effects
Noise Pollution	
Causes	Effects

5. Long answer questions.

a. What is pollution? What are the various types of pollution?

____

____

b. How is air pollution harmful to us?

____

____

c. Why is land pollution unhealthy for the soil?

____

____

d. How is noise pollution harmful to us?

____

____

6. Think and write

Segregation of waste is practiced nowadays to differentiate biodegradable and non-biodegradable waste. Think of the ways in which we can reuse or recycle household waste.

____

____

____

____

7. Activity time

Explore and find the diseases which occur due to different types of pollution. Make a detailed project on the same with the help of the data collected by you.

Natural Phenomena

1. Fill in the blanks.

a. After reaching the surface, the magma is called ______________.

b. An ______________ volcano can erupt at any time.

c. The location inside the Earth where the earthquake begins is called the ______________.

d. A ______________ is used to measure the strength of a tremor.

e. Droughts occur due to lack of ______________.

2. Write T for true statements and F for false ones.

a. Earthquakes cannot occur under the sea. ☐

b. Floods happen due to shortage of rain. ☐

c. The heat from the lava of a volcano can cause fire. ☐

d. A dormant volcano is not expected to erupt again. ☐

e. A vent is a crack in the crust of the Earth. ☐

3. Name the following.

a. The topmost layer of the Earth. ______________

b. The innermost layer of the Earth. ______________

c. The point under the Earth where a quake begins. ______________

d. Middle layer of the Earth. ______________

e. Hollow opening at the top of a volcano. ______________

4. Match the following.

Column A	Column B
a. Shock waves	Seismograph
b. Tidal waves	Volcanic eruption
c. Magma	Tsunami
d. Richter scale	Cooled magma
e. Lava	Earthquake

5. Short answer questions.

a. What is a natural disaster?

____

b. Why do earthquakes occur?

____

c. What is magma?

____

d. What is a cyclone?

____

e. What does a seismograph measure?

____

f. What are some natural causes of forest fires?

____

6. Long answer questions.

a. What are the effects of an earthquake?

____

____

b. What is a volcano? What is the major cause of a volcanic eruption?

____

____

c. Explain the three types of volcanoes.

____

____

d. What is a tsunami? Why are they caused?

____

____

e. What is the difference between a flood and a drought?

____

____

7. Think and write

Most of the countries of the world are dealing with floods and droughts. Think and write ways to help the people dealing with these disasters.

____

____

____

____

____

8. Activity time

Find out the safety measures that should be taken in case of an earthquake. Which disaster management systems and tools are adopted by your school for safety in case of an earthquake or fire?

The Earth, Sun and Moon

1. Answer the following in one word.

a. A huge ball of hot and burning gases. ____________________

b. The phase of the moon when it is not visible. ____________________

c. The name for the eclipse of the moon. ____________________

d. The name for the eclipse of the sun. ____________________

e. Deep holes on the surface of the moon. ____________________

2. Match the following.

Column A	Column B
a. Craters	Outermost part of the sun's atmosphere
b. Ozone layer	Molten rocks in Earth's mantle
c. Corona	Protective layer of Earth
d. Magma	Surface of the moon

3. Short answer questions.

a. What lies on the outermost layer of the Earth?

____

b. What is corona?

____

c. Name two types of eclipses.

____

d. Define phases of the moon.

____

e. Who was the first astronaut to land on the moon?

____

f. What is an artificial satellite?

____

4. Long answer questions.

a. Describe the various layers of the Earth.

____

____

b. Write a short note to describe the sun.

____

____

c. What is an eclipse? How are they caused?

____

____

d. What are carters? How are they formed?

____

____

5. **Draw a labelled diagram showing the different phases of the moon in the space below.**

6. **Draw a labelled diagram showing the various layers of the Earth. Also write two things that can be found in each layer.**

7. **Think and write**

No sound can be heard on the moon. Why do you think it is so? Think and write your ideas. (Remember how sound travels)

____

____

____

____

____

8. **Activity time**

Use a torch and balls of various sizes to make a model of the eclipse. Use this model to explain how an eclipse occurs.

The Solar System

1. Fill in the blanks.

a. All the planets ______________ around the sun.

b. Mars is also known as the ______________ planet.

c. Saturn is at ______________ position from the sun.

d. All the planets get heat and light from the ______________.

e. ______________ reflects the light of the sun on the Earth.

2. Write T for true statements and F for false ones.

a. The gravity on moon is more than that on the Earth. ☐

b. Venus is the hottest planet of our solar system. ☐

c. Saturn has many rings around it. ☐

d. Earth takes one day to orbit the sun. ☐

e. Moon is an artificial satellite. ☐

3. Match the following.

Column A	**Column B**
a. Natural satellite	Saturn
b. Artificial satellite	Pluto
c. Dwarf planet	Aryabhata
d. Planet with maximum rings	Sun
e. Star	Moon

4. Short answer questions.

a. How many planets are there in our solar system?

____

b. Which planet is nearest to the sun?

____

c. Which planet is farthest from the sun?

____

d. Which is the largest planet?

____

e. Which is the smallest planet?

____

f. What is a satellite?

____

5. Long answer questions.

a. What are the different types of heavenly bodies in our solar system?

____

____

b. How is the Earth different from other planets?

____

____

c. What are dwarf planets? Name three dwarf planets.

d. How is Saturn different from other planets of the solar system?

6. Think and write

Do you think there is a possibility of life on any planet other than Earth?

7. Activity time

Visit the official website of NASA and collect information about the recent Mars mission. Make a presentation showing the importance and findings of the mission.

Answers

Growing Plants

1. a. seeds b. crops
   c. mountains d. cotyledons
   e. dispersal
2. a. T b. F c. F d. T e. F
3. a. 4 b. 1 c. 2 d. 5 e. 3
4. a. Seed b. Eyes
   c. Stem d. Roots
   e. Leaf
5. a. Peas, Beans b. Cottonwood, Dandelion
   c. Cherry, Apple d. Coconut, Lotus

Animals and Their Features

1. a. Carnivores b. freshwater habitat
   c. scales d. Ocean
   e. coastal
2. a. F b. T c. F d. F e. T
3. a. Snail, Nautilus, Tortoise
   b. Porcupine, Hedgehog, Echidna
   c. Bear, Rabbit, Sheep
   d. Crow, Flamingo, Hen
   e. Penguin, Turtle, Dolphin
4. a. Camel, Addax antelope
   b. Whales, Octopus
   c. Elephant, Giraffe
   d. Penguin, Seal
   e. Mountain goat, Cougar

Skeletal System

1. a. Skull b. Pivotal
   c. Bone marrow d. Tendons
   e. Girdle
2. a. F b. T c. F d. F
3. a. Rib cage
   b. Vertebral column
   c. Two girdles
   d. Inside the backbone
   e. Ball and socket joint
   f. Hinge joint
   g. Ligaments tissues connect two bones.
4. a. Back and Forth Movement
   b. Elbow joint
   c. Connects the head to the neck
   d. Joints in our wrist

Nervous System

1. a. Cerebrum b. Hair
   c. Spinal cord d. Medulla
   e. Nerves
2. a. T b. T c. F d. F
4. a. Pupil b. Skin
   c. Eardrum d. Nostrils
   e. Taste buds

Food and Health

1. a. Cereals b. Measles
   c. Goitre d. Corns
   e. Vaccine
2. a. F b. F c. T d. F e. T
3. a. Correct b. clean
   c. stagnant d. unhealthy
   e. uncovered
4. a. Deficiency of Vitamin C, Orange; lemons and strawberries
   b. Deficiency of Vitamin B-1; Milk, cereals and leafy vegetables
   c. Deficiency of Vitamin A; Egg, milk and green leafy vegetables
   d. Deficiency of Iron; Spinach, Beans, Apple and Tofu
   e. Deficiency of Iodine; Iodized salt, meat and seafood

Safety and First-Aid

1. a. fracture b. doctor
   c. snake d. sand
   e. gas leakage
2. a. F b. T c. T d. T e. F
3. a. Fire extinguisher
   b. First-Aid
   c. Baking soda or toothpaste
   d. Splint
   e. Ice pack

Rocks and Minerals

1. a. Core b. Obsidian
   c. Sandstone d. Limestone
   e. Iron
2. a. T b. F c. F d. T e. T
3. a. Pumice, Granite, Obsidian
   b. Sandstone, Shale, Limestone
   c. Marble, Slate, Gneiss
   d. Iron, Magnetite, Bauxite
   e. Coal, Mica, Dolamite
4. a. Thin layers of solidified clay
   b. Formed from granite
   c. Rich in mineral quartz
   d. Hard rock formed by lava

e. Porous rock

Light and Shadow

1. a. opaque b. light
   c. black d. Sun
   e. short
2. Luminous: torch, lamp, sun, fire
   Non-luminous: wooden chair, plastic bottle, water, mirror
4. a. Sun, Lamp
   b. Book, Tree
   c. Clear glass, Air
   d. Oiled paper, Coloured glass
   e. Wall, Rock

Force

1. a. move b. shape
   c. Oil d. gravitational
   e. opposite
2. a. T b. F c. F d. T e. F
3. a. Fruits falling on the ground.
   b. Reducing speed of a rolling ball.
   c. The needle of a compass.
   d. The movement of cobs of a machine.
   e. A ball floating on the water.
4. a. slows down movement
   b. Used to attract metals
   c. Pulling force of the Earth
   d. Push or pull
   e. Upward force

Energy

1. a. heat b. geothermal
   c. electrical d. first-class
   e. light
2. a. F b. T c. T d. F e. T
3. a. Solar energy, Geothermal energy
   b. Energy from coal, Petroleum
   c. Scissor, Sea-saw
   d. Nut cracker, Wheelbarrow
   e. Arm, Fishing rod
   f. Knife, Axe
   g. Light bulb, Lid of a jar
   h. Ramp, Wedges
4. a. Hydro energy
   b. Wind energy
   c. Solar energy
   d. Sound energy

e. Electrical energy

Environmental Pollution

1. a. air b. water
   c. ears d. deforestation
   e. fossil
2. a. F b. T c. F d. F e. T

Natural Phenomena

1. a. lava b. active
   c. focus d. seismograph
   e. rain
2. a. F b. F c. T d. F e. T
3. a. Crust b. Core
   c. Focus d. Mantle
   e. Crater
4. a. Earthquake
   b. Tsunami
   c. Volcanic eruption
   d. Seismograph
   e. Cooled magma

The Earth, Sun and Moon

1. a. Sun
   b. New moon
   c. Lunar eclipse
   d. Solar eclipse
   e. Craters
2. a. Surface of the moon
   b. Protective layer of the Earth
   c. Outermost part of the sun's atmosphere
   d. Molten rocks in Earth's mantle

The Solar System

1. a. revolve
   b. red
   c. sixth
   d. sun
   e. Moon
2. a. F b. T c. T d. F e. F
3. a. Moon
   b. Aryabhata
   c. Pluto
   d. Saturn
   e. Sun